God's Love Raised Me

A Testimony Of God's Love Fathering The Fatherless.

Eric Richards

PREFACE

"God's Love Raised Me" is more than a memoir; it's a vivid journey through the highs and lows of life, colored with resilience and triumph. I was immersed in the world of challenges and adversity from the earliest moments of my life. I could have let those challenges define my path. Instead, leaning on God's love and trusting his path guided me to an unexplainable life.

This book chronicles my journey from a challenged childhood to a place of stability and deliverance. This story depicts growth, relentless pursuit of a better self and perseverance. I learned invaluable lessons about responsibility, and the pure essence of living a purposeful life.

Each chapter reveals the lessons learned, the battles fought, and the victories won, all rooted in the timeless values of faith, accountability, endurance, and being optimistic. I invite you to embark on this journey with me, to find inspiration in every situation we find ourselves, and to discover the boundless potential that lies within you. I hope that each page of this book will inspire and encourage you to navigate your own challenges with courage and grace, knowing that God will always be there with you every step of the way.

Every challenge I faced was a lesson in resilience while holding unto God's unchanging hand. Through each trial, I discovered the power of God's Love and the importance of trusting him. I learned that setbacks are not the end, but a journey to something greater.

As I grew and matured, so did my understanding of what it means to be blessed and highly favored. I faced each situation head-on, armed with the wisdom imparted by the elders in my family and in my community. Through God's grace, all the tribulations I faced in life became testimonies on my journey to becoming the Man I am today.

"God's Love Raised Me" is a call to action, not just my story. It serves as a reminder that each of us holds the potential to overcome challenges, transform, and attain greatness. "God's Love Raised Me" invites you to reflect on your own lives, trust in God in the face of adversity, and break through every barrier that stands in your way.

I hope as you read through this book, you will find it as a source of hope and inspiration. Let my story remind you that there's always a way forward. Ensure to embrace the principles that guide you, cherish the lessons learned, and never underestimate the power of faith. God's Love will never fail.

FORWARD

With excitement, it's an honor to introduce "God's Love Raised Me," a profoundly moving and inspiring autobiography by Eric Richards. In this noteworthy book, Eric Richards calls us into the private story of his childhood, sharing the pivotal moments and lessons that shaped his resilient spirit and unwavering determination.

From the beginning, Eric Richards' lack of parental presence in his life was marked by challenges that would have daunted many. Thank God for the other family members around him who instilled a sense of faith that became the cornerstone of his success. It is evident that his journey to success was fueled by the power of an unyielding spirit that refuses to be weighed down by the adversities of life.

"God's Love Raised Me" is not a recounting of childhood events; it is a powerful narrative of growth, courage, and relentless pursuit of one's potential. Eric Richards' story passes for an inspiration to all who face difficulties, letting us know that with the right mindset, we can adapt and overcome.

As you read through the pages of this book, set your mind to be uplifted and motivated by his extraordinary life story. Every page is filled with candid reflections and life lessons that are both poignant and profoundly inspirational. I am sure his experiences and insights will resonate deeply, offering hope and encouragement to everyone striving to navigate their own journeys.

ACKNOWLEDGEMENT

This book is dedicated to my mother, Ladedra Henley, and my grandmother, Virginia Scott, who've gone home to be with the Lord. The way I was raised in the '80s resembles the way many have been brought up today. My Grandmother took on the responsibility of raising me, not only as her grandson but as her son, and I'm forever grateful. I also want to acknowledge my aunt, Bexzina Jordan, who assisted in ensuring I had what I needed to live a normal life amid the circumstances laid before me as a child. I want to thank my lovely wife, Daphne Richards, for the push and encouragement to stand and proclaim what God has done in my life.

Lastly, I want to acknowledge Rev. George Horne, Mother Louise Horne, Pastor Scott Sanders, and Co-Pastor Cynthia Sanders for the introduction of whom God is in his word and the love they've shown me. Because of their love, leadership, and care for me as a Spiritual Son, I'm now able to bear fruit and make the testimony of my life tangible and visible. It is my desire that others may be encouraged and inspired by the testimony log of my youth.

Your past victories could be someone else's vision to free them from their present chains. God, I give you all the glory, and I thank you for keeping my memory intact so that I can pour out and capture the testimonies in this book to bless the nations.

TABLE OF CONTENTS

Acknowledgement I

Chapter 1: Born Abroad, Raised in the US. 1

Chapter 2: The Chosen One 14

Chapter 3: Birth Records Mistakenly Forsaken 25

Chapter 4: What Does Death Mean? 34

Chapter 5: Appreciation in the Midst of Poverty 43

Chapter 6: I Can't Go for That 54

Chapter 7: Close Your Eyes and Make Believe 60

Chapter 8: The Power of Worship 68

Chapter 9: There's No Place Like Home 76

Chapter 10: Time is Winding Down 86

Chapter 11: Grace and Favor 100

Chapter 12: God Brought Me Out 110

Isaiah 49:15 (NLV)
"Can a woman forget her nursing child? Can she have no pity on the son to whom she gave birth? Even these may forget, but I will not forget you.

In Memory Of My Grandmother
Virginia Scott

CHAPTER 1
Born Abroad, Raised in the US.

My mother and father were from two different worlds. My mother was born in Quitman, Georgia, while my father is a native of Hickory, North Carolina. Fate would have it that they both joined the United States Army and were stationed in Seoul, Korea. I was born on November 26, 1980, at the 121 US Army Hospital in South Korea. There's no remembrance of the flight to the United States, which leaves me curious, as God has blessed me to remember almost every moment of my life.

The day was December 25, 1982. My father unloaded me out of the back seat of his car and brought me into my grandmother Virginia's house in Adel, Georgia. As we entered her home, he sat me down on a beautiful white floor and gave me a toy to play with. As I looked up at him, I saw him talking with my grandmother. This was the first time in my life I heard a still voice give me comfort and guidance simultaneously. In my heart, I heard, "He's about to leave you here, so let's crawl around."

As I was crawling, I heard gunshots and horses, which immediately got my attention. When I crawled into this room, there was a man sitting on the edge of the bed wearing brown trousers and a white t-shirt. He picked me up off the floor, sat me in bed with him, and began playing with me. The first thing I noticed were the funny shaped cookies he had, and he offered me a few. As I was watching westerns with him, I went to sleep on his chest. I woke up and gazed at him, wondering if he would leave me just like my father did. But instead, he looked back at me and embraced me like I was his son, and I felt like he was my dad.

As I began to grow, he started referring to me as "Big Boy!" He was a truck driver and worked on different farms from time to time.

"Big Boy, you want to go with me to feed the cows?"

"Yes, Sir," I would always say.

He would also take me on the road with him to deliver produce from the farm to other stores around

South Georgia. As I was sitting on the passenger side of the truck, I would stare out the window and feel the love in my heart from being around my dad. Even though he was my grandmother's boyfriend, to me, he was my dad. He and my grandmother showed me what it was like to have a mother and a father in the home.

One night, they decided to go out and leave me slumbering in bed. When I woke up, it was late, and they were nowhere to be found. I remembered my dad taking me to and from his mother's house, Mrs. Rosa Strickland, which was 5 minutes away. So, I grabbed my bottle and walked to her house in the middle of the night. I knocked on the door, and immediately the porch lit up with the light of curiosity. When she opened the door, she looked down and saw me looking up at her with my bottle in my hand. She became nurturing and furious at the same time. She brought me into her house, poured some milk into my bottle, and settled me in bed with her. After I finished drinking, I would let the bottle fall to the floor, and she would pick it up and refill it. I did this a second time, and she warned, "If you drop it again, it's staying on the floor."

The next morning, there was banging at the door. My Grandmother Rosa, which is what our relationship grew to be, rushed me back into my dad's room. She told me, "Don't make any noise; I will come and get you." I heard my grandmother and dad crying because they couldn't find me and didn't know where I was. I heard Grandmother Rosa say, "I haven't seen him." I was smiling because I knew she had seen me. I'm right here! She made them experience the pain of being careless and irresponsible guardians. She told them, "I don't know where he is, but you all better go find him, or I'm calling the police." They cried even harder, as they walked out the front door to search for me. I then heard her say, "Lafayette, go look in your room; he's in there." I heard him rushing towards me, and when he saw me in bed, he picked me up and grabbed me so tightly. I was very happy to see my dad. From that point on, my grandmother never let me out of her sight.

They took what Grandma Rosa said to heart because the next week, things got really interesting for me. It was nighttime, and my grandmother loaded me up in the back of her 1980 Red Lincoln Continental with the red leather seats. And we're off!

We got to this big wooden house known as Witt Lanes, which had loud music coming from it. She unloaded me and brought me into the house with her. When she opened the door, the music got louder, and I didn't know what was going on. All I remember hearing was, "P-L-A-Y, if you play with me, it's at your risk, and I'll set you free." She sat me down up front with a woman and gave me some Lays Plain Chips with a Coca-Cola. The lady up front made sure I was okay as my grandmother went to enjoy herself with her friends. I wasn't afraid or upset. I was excited! I didn't know what was happening, but my grandmother came back every few minutes to check on me and ensure I had all the Lays Chips I could eat.

Saturday mornings were routine. She would turn on Soul Train and start cleaning the house. She would walk me into the bathroom, sit me on her lap, and train me to brush my own teeth. At 4 years old, I helped her clean the house, pick up paper in the yard, and dust the wooden shelf that my uncle had built for her living room. The most impactful moments were when I would do what she trained me to do. When I finished the tasks, she would review what I'd done and smile, saying, "You did a really good job dusting and sweeping. You're growing up!" My eyes and heart would light up every time she would give me affirmations. I would look for things to do because I knew she would be proud of me.

"Chip?"

"Yes, ma'am," I answered.

"Come into the kitchen and get ready for breakfast!"

She would make cheese grits, salmon croquette patties, and biscuits, which I feared when she opened them. Each time she opened those cans of biscuits, it was as if a gunshot had been fired. After breakfast, she would allow me to go outside and play. In the '80s, kids were always outside playing every Saturday morning in my neighborhood. There were kids racing, playing football, and having fun on one end of the street. On the other end of the street were guys with drinks covered with plastic bags, boom boxes on their shoulders, with a lot of trash talking going on. This street, which was known as Sesame

Street, was right next to our house. The more we played and spent time with each other, the more we became like brothers and sisters from different mothers.

There was a local candy shop in our neighborhood called Cookie Man. This place provided all types of cookies, candies, drinks, and even a barbershop. After exhausting all my energy playing with my friends, I would run home and ask my grandmother for 50 cents. I would go and buy chocolate chip cookies with a soda every time. One of my dad's friends standing on the corner would always ask me, "Hey boy, what you got in that bag?"

"Chocolate chip cookies," I replied.

"Let me get a couple of those."

I would immediately reach into my bag, give him two cookies, and skip away. Every time I went to the cookie store, the same guy would be on the corner of the street and ask, "Hey boy, what you got in that bag?"

"Chocolate chip cookies," I would always reply.

"You know what, we're going to start calling you Chip because every time we see you, you got a bag of chocolate chip cookies. Now, let me get two of them cookies."

I reached into my bag and gave him two cookies, and he gave me one dollar. I ran home and told my grandmother what the man said, and she agreed. From that day forward, I was known in the neighborhood as Chip.

I spent a lot of time hanging around older people. My grandmother's house was the place where people came to laugh and have a good time. One day, two men began arguing in my grandmother's house while the music was playing, and everyone was enjoying themselves. Suddenly, the music stopped, and I heard a loud voice.

"Look ah here, man! I love you, but you're dead wrong, and you know it."

"You're right, man; I'm sorry," the other guy replied.

The music started playing again, and I would see those same two men getting along as if the situation never happened. Back then, when people had disagreements, they would address the situation right away and get back to having fun as if it never happened.

The hot summer months brought much excitement to our home and curiosity in me as a kid. Our relatives traveled from Miami, Florida, Daytona Beach, Florida, and Quitman, Georgia to visit us. I recall thinking that these were potential friends, but I would learn what it meant to have cousins.

While the beauty of life, loving family and friends were unfolding before me, some moments shook me to my core. There were nights when I would be awakened to the sounds of fighting and arguing. I was able to make sense of those situations during those times.

You see, despite the love my grandmother, dad, and many of our family and friends shared, alcohol often took its toll, leading to disputes that affected their relationships with one another.

One night, I woke up to my grandmother and dad fighting. I rushed out of bed and went to the living room and peeped around the corner. My dad pushed my grandmother to the floor. Suddenly, she got up, grabbed a glass bottle, broke it on the top of his head, and pushed him out the screen door. She slammed the door as if it was a gavel in the courtroom. Once she slammed the door, I ran and jumped back in the bed as if I didn't know what was going on. She came into my room and got me out of bed. I was so scared because my grandmother's clothes were ripped, and she had glass in her beautiful black hair with tears running down her face.

"Get up and come with me," she said.

She grabbed me by the hand, took me into the bathroom, let the seat lid down on the toilet, and sat me down.

"Look at me, Chip," she said. "I want you to look in the mirror and see yourself." She said, "You're a handsome little boy, do you know that?"

I started smiling and replied, "Yes, ma'am."

She looked me straight in my eyes and said these words, "You're going to grow up to be a handsome young man. Don't you ever put your hands on a woman because you don't have to. If you feel like you have to hit a woman, you leave her! Do you understand me?"

"Yes, ma'am," I replied.

"Good. Now, go get back in the bed," she said.

I was no longer focused on the fear of what just happened, but I was focusing on what she said and glad that the fight was finally over.

Days would go by, and I noticed that my dad wasn't around. This was the first time that I had grown to miss someone. No matter what negative emotion or feeling I had, whenever I would see my grandmother's smile, I knew everything would be alright. Suddenly, there was a knock at the door.

"Who is it?" my grandmother said.

"Lafayette," my dad responded.

She walked to the door, let him in, and they hugged each other. I was sitting on the couch watching because I didn't know if she was going to hit him on the head with a bottle again. When I saw them smiling, I ran into the kitchen towards my dad, and he picked me up! The feeling of missing my dad went away instantly. He put me on his back, walked me all the way to The Cookie Man, and bought me anything I wanted that day. Afterwards, he took me to his mother's house. She had long silver hair and a smile that would always bring heaven to earth. She always kept the Bible near her rocking chair. She sat me on her lap, read scriptures, and ministered to me.

"Chip, make sure you always do the right thing, baby," she said. "You see how those men be drinking on the corner?"

"Yes, ma'am," I replied.

"That's not the right thing to do, and you should stay away from that stuff."

The lessons I received at this age were before my time, but when I look back on them, they were seeds that were planted for my protection. I was around older people all the time. God always supplied someone in my life to sow seeds in my heart as a child to ensure I was raised the right way.

CHAPTER 2
The Chosen One

In 1984, my mother was stationed in Colorado upon returning from Korea. When she returned to Adel, she had two new sons: Carlos, who was two years old, and Terrance, a newborn. I remember when she laid them before my Grandmother Virginia, and how excited she was to see them.

"These are your brothers, Eric!" my mother, Ladedra said.

As a kid, I didn't know what that meant; I just wanted to play with them. Carlos was just like me! He was very energetic and curious about things. I remember him walking, stumbling, crawling, laughing, and starting all over again. We would play all day until we were worn out. Grandma would feed us, put us to bed, and we repeated the process the next day. Carlos always looked up to me, and I made sure to set an example of goodness before him.

We never got a chance to play with Terrance because he was so young. We would look at him in the crib, smiling and cooing without a care in the world. When the adults would come over, we had to go to another room and play. During this time, children were not allowed to be in the same room as adults when they were talking.

"Chip and Terrance, y'all go back in the middle room and play." My Grandmother Virginia said.

Yes, ma'am," we said.

We went into the room, jumped on the bed, and played. We would lay on the floor and play with the little green army men our mother gave us. We played war for so long that it eventually lost its thrill for me. I became so bored that I got creative. I thought to myself, they are going to pay us some attention today.

"Terrance, stay right here; I'll be right back," I said to my brother.

I crept into the kitchen, got the bag of all-purpose flour, and brought it back into the room. I smeared the flour on my face, like the cartoons we would see on *Tom and Jerry*. Terrance began to laugh at me, and I remember the feeling of bringing joy to my little brother.

"You want some on your face, too?"

"Yeah," he replied.

I took the flour and smeared it on his face, and we both began to laugh at each other! The front room was filled with adults listening to music and enjoying themselves. I took him by the hand and walked him through the colorful beads and into the front room.

Immediately, everyone in the front room began laughing at us very loudly.

"What in the world is this?" Grandmother Rosa said as she laughed.

I took the chance of us getting into trouble because I wanted to be around my grandmother, Virginia. Laughingly, my grandmother, Virginia, said, "Chip, ain't nobody did this but you."

"Virginia, we got to take a picture of this," grandmother Rosa said.

My grandmother, Virginia, rushed off to her room to get her Polaroid camera. She came back into the kitchen, reached into the cabinet, and grabbed new film cartridges for her camera. Grandmother Rosa sat us on her lap at the kitchen table, while my Grandmother Virginia, took a picture of me and Carlos with flour on our faces. After the picture, grandmother Rosa sat at the table while we were on her lap and laughed at what we had done.

"Can we keep it on?" I asked.

"No, you can't, Chip," grandmother Rosa said. "Go in the bathroom, get a wet rag, and wipe that off your face and Carlos' face."

As the days went by, we continued to bond together as brothers. We would sit on the floor and watch *Reading Rainbow*, *Muppet Babies*, *Mister Rogers' Neighborhood*, and other educational shows. My grandmother, Virginia, was very particular about what we watched on television. While my grandmother and dad would go to work, she would have someone come over and watch us during the day until my Aunt Bexzina got out of school.

My aunt was a typical '80s teen, wearing colorful leather jackets, jerry curls, acid wash jeans, and having many friends. My aunt and uncles Fred and Verdette were very fond of my brothers and me. They would always play with us and make us laugh when they had the time. They were always on the go.

One day, my mother, Ladedra, came home and began to pack up my brothers' and my things. I became sad because it seemed as if we were getting ready to leave the place that I had grown to love these past five years. Once she was done packing, she sat all three of us on the couch and began loading our bags in the car.

As she was loading us up, my grandmother, Virginia, walked into the house from her lunch break. I jumped off the couch and ran to her. I grabbed her but didn't let her go.

"What are you doing, Ladedra?" she asked her daughter.

"I'm going to take the boys and give them up for adoption," she replied.

My mother began to cry, and I was so afraid because I didn't want to leave my grandmother.

"You can take Carlos and Terrance, but Chip is staying here," my grandmother said.

My mother, Ladedra, took my brothers and loaded them up in the car, leaving me behind with my grandmother. I stood at the screen door, watching my grandmother Virginia in tears as my mother drove off with my brothers. That was the last time I saw them. My grandmother came into the house and prepared me a fried bologna sandwich while the babysitter looked on in disbelief. I ate my sandwich, got on the couch, and took a nap. When I woke up, I remember the hurt I felt from not being able to play with my brothers. I was confused as to what had happened. As the days went by, I totally forgot about what happened because I spent a lot of time playing in the street with my friends.

It was December 24, 1985, and I was excited about Santa Claus coming to bring me gifts. My grandmother had a tree with red and green lights at the front door. During Christmas time, she made sure the front door stayed locked and that no one came into that entrance.

"Grandma, is Santa Claus coming to our house tonight?" I asked.

"I don't know, but you better make sure he has some milk and cookies just in case," she said.

I didn't have any money, so I asked my dad for 50 cents, and he gave me $2.00! I felt like I was rich! I made sure to go by Cookie Man's to get Santa Claus some chocolate chip cookies, strawberry cookies, and oatmeal windmill cookies for good measure! I left a brown paper bag of cookies and milk on the table after everyone went to bed that night.

I woke up the next morning and rushed to the Christmas tree. My Aunt Bexzina, grandmother Rosa, grandmother Virginia, and my dad Lafayette were already in the living room around the Christmas tree. The first thing I saw was a red candy apple bike with training wheels on it.

"Daddy, is this mine?" I asked.

"Yes, it got your name on it," he replied.

I was so excited that I asked if I could go outside and ride it right now!

"Open the rest of your gifts and see what Santa brought you," my dad replied.

I looked up at my grandmother Virginia as she smiled at me with so much joy in her eyes. Once I finished opening my gifts, I put on my brand-new clothes that my grandmother Rosa and my grandmother Virginia bought me for Christmas. My grandmother put a hood on my head, and my dad helped me take my bike outside. It was a beautiful day on Sesame Street. Everyone was riding their bikes, dressed in new clothes, playing with new toys, and smiling.

My dad began to train me to ride my new bicycle. As the days went by, he would challenge me to ride faster.

"It's time for you to learn how to ride without training wheels," he said.

He took off the training wheels and guided me into riding the bike without them. I remember the excitement he had once I achieved riding a bicycle on my own. It was important for him to see me accomplishing what he had trained me to do. As I gained more confidence, I would go joyriding with my friends.

"Dad, can I ride my bike to the field and play football with my friends?" I asked.

"Yes, but you better be home by the time that streetlight comes on," he replied.

My friends and I had a great time playing football on the field. As the evening progressed, I lost track of time, and suddenly, all the streetlights came on at the same time. I got on my bike and rode home as fast as I could. When I got home, my dad was waiting for me in the kitchen.

"Didn't I tell you to be home by the time that streetlight came on?" he said.

"Yes, sir," I replied.

He calmly told me to follow him to the bedroom. He took off his belt, laid me on his lap, and spanked me with his belt. It was the most painful thing I had ever experienced. After I was done crying from that treacherous spanking, he looked me in the eyes and told me, "When I tell you to do something, do it!" This was the first time my dad disciplined me, but it sure wasn't the last.

When I was disobedient around the house, my dad would make me lie on the floor and hold my legs up in the air for hours. My legs would begin to burn, and I would start to cry because my stomach muscles were burning.

"Lafayette, he's been down there long enough. Let him up," my grandmother Virginia said.

After he let me up, I rushed to my grandmother so she could console me.

"Get off me and go over there and sit down. I'm not going to baby you when you're doing the wrong thing," she said.

At that moment, I learned that my grandmother would never bail me out of trouble if I was wrong. She was passionate about me developing integrity and not being babied.

CHAPTER 3
Birth Records Mistakenly Forsaken

After the summer of 1985, my grandmother Virginia enrolled me in a daycare that was a few minutes from our house and right across the street from her job. I was excited about being able to attend school. I was prepared to put into practice everything that I'd learned from watching GPTV at home every day.

The next day, my grandmother took me to the school to complete the enrollment process, only to be told by a staff member that they had lost my birth certificate. This incident at school would mark the beginning of a difficult journey for me as a child.

The next day, my grandmother Virginia went to the courthouse to inform the clerk's office of the situation and to gain assistance. The courthouse couldn't provide any records or assist us with my issue due to my birth being abroad, and no records of my birth were filed in Cook County. The only support they could provide was phone numbers and addresses for the U.S. Embassy.

"Until I can get a copy of your birth certificate, you're coming to work with me," my grandmother said.

I was disappointed and excited! The next morning, my grandmother woke me up and instructed me to get dressed.

"Make sure you make your bed up before you come out of that room," she said.

Once I completed my tasks, I would eat the breakfast she prepared and watch television until it was time to go. I remember watching Gil Patrick on *Today in Georgia* every morning.

"Chip, turn the TV off, and let's go!" she said.

We were on our way on foot to her job, known as Del-Cook, which was a thriving lumber yard business in our community.

"Virginia, where is Chip going early this morning?" her friend asked.

"He's coming with me since they lost his birth certificate at the preschool," she replied.

I would be on the lumber line with all the adults. Even though I was a child, they still treated me like I was one of the workers. I recall trying to pick up wood to give to my mother for the chainsaw.

"You can't do that here," she said. "I know you want to help, but just stand by me."

I would watch other men and women work. They were amazed and puzzled to see a 5-year-old on the lumber line with them, when I should've been at school. During the break, I would sit and eat the meal that my grandmother prepared for me. From time to time, some of the folks would stop and have a conversation with me about why I wasn't at school.

My grandmother would repeat the same thing to everyone. I could tell she was getting frustrated, even though she didn't show it. A few hours later, a loud horn blew. It was known as the 12:00 whistle. Immediately, everyone dropped the wood at their stations and began to rush downstairs to ground level. Some people would get on their bikes, others would rush to their cars, and the rest would quickly walk home for their one-hour lunch break.

I spent a few months going back and forth to work with my grandmother at Del-Cook. Some days, I would ride with my dad when he would deliver produce to other cities. One day, the supervisor informed my grandmother that I could no longer be at work with her and that she would have to find a babysitter.

The next morning, I remember waking up early and being picked up by someone I've never seen.

"Chip," my grandmother said, "you're going to stay with Carolyn while I work today. Ensure you do the right thing and don't get into trouble."

My grandmother had one of her friends drop me off with someone she trusted. Once I got to the babysitter's house, she had a big smile on her face and was very welcoming. She prepared me a pallet on the floor next to a beautiful but scary fish tank. There were other kids scattered around on the floor as well. Immediately, I was ready to go back home! This was the first time I was away from my grandmother for a long period of time.

"Come on in and lay down," she said.

I laid down on the floor and quietly cried myself to sleep. I really wanted to be at the lumber yard with my grandmother and her friends. I was now experiencing what it was like to be around other children and to be raised by someone other than my grandmother.

"Time to wake up!" Mrs. Carolyn said.

She prepared us breakfast while she played educational programs on television. Once we were done, she gave us books to read.

"Chip, do you know how to read?" she asked.

"No, ma'am," I replied.

She would help me sound out words and teach me the meaning of those words. I grew to appreciate Mrs. Carolyn day after day. She would teach me about colors, animals, sounds, and other foundational information that I was getting behind on.

One of the main things I learned from Mrs. Carolyn is the importance of wearing socks with cowboy boots. One morning, my grandmother allowed me to dress myself before my ride came to pick me up. I decided to put on a white shirt, some jeans, and cowboy boots with no socks on. I was trying to emulate the men that I would see around me and on TV.

Once I got to her house, it was time to lay down as usual. I took off my cowboy boots.

"Chip, is that your feet smelling like that?" she asked.

"I don't know," I replied.

"Put the boots back on and lay down. You don't wear shoes without socks, baby," she said.

That was the first time I was embarrassed because my feet smelled very offensive to her and the students in her home.

During the fall of 1986, my grandmother tried to enroll me in kindergarten. I remember my grandmother sitting across from the principal of the school in her office. She explained to the principal that I didn't have a birth certificate or a social security number.

"I've been trying to get his birth certificate from the U.S. Embassy, and I haven't heard anything back for the past two years," my grandmother said.

"Ms. Virginia, we can't let him sit out of school forever," the principal said. "We will let him attend school. You will have to bring us his records as soon as you get them. He can start tomorrow," the principal stated.

My grandmother was so excited because I could now start school! My grandmother and I walked from Adel Elementary School to a store called Allied. She purchased me some clothes, pencils, paper, a backpack, shoes, and a welcome home mat. I didn't know what the mat was for, but I was excited to have it.

The next day when I got to school, I met my kindergarten teacher, Mrs. Bradford. We prayed and said the Pledge of Allegiance before class started. I turned in my mat to my teacher. I would later discover that the mats were for naptime. All the other kids had red and blue rubber mats. I was curled up on my welcome home mat like a cat and was content just like the other kids, even though they all laughed at me. I didn't care at all because my grandmother bought it for me, and I was thankful for it.

As teaching was going forward, I was being a distraction because I thought I could talk anytime I wanted to, as I did when I was on the lumber line with my grandmother and her friends. I learned very quickly that you must follow the rules and listen to succeed in school.

Later that year, I celebrated my 6th birthday. My Grandmother Rosa bought me a gray suit, black shoes, and a Cabbage Patch Kid Hat. This was the first birthday party I'd ever had. My aunt bought me an ice cream cake and some shoes. They took a picture of me in the suit with the Cabbage Patch Kid Hat on my head.

I stood with my hands behind my back and didn't show my teeth as I smiled because something was missing. I was missing my brothers and was confused about why I hadn't seen my dad in a while. Nevertheless, I was still thankful for having my first birthday party.

CHAPTER 4
What Does Death Mean?

The year was 1988, and my second-grade school year was coming to a close. I remember drawing a picture for my dad at the end of school and being excited to give it to him. I got off the bus and ran into the house.

"Momma, look what I drew for Daddy! Can I give it to him?" I asked.

"Chip, Lafayette died this morning at the hospital in Gainesville," she said.

I didn't know what "died" meant, but it didn't sound good. I remember leaning on the wall in the kitchen when she told me the news. I didn't cry or feel any emotion. I didn't know what it meant.

I remember going to bed that night and thinking to myself, "I can't wait to see Daddy tomorrow." As the days went by, there were a lot of people coming over to our house with food and sad faces. Every time the screen door opened, I would look to see if he was coming in the door, but he never showed up.

My grandmother's sister, Mattlyn, came and picked us up in her Crimson Red Chevy Caprice and took us back to Quitman with her. I was sitting in the back seat, and my grandmother began to sing the gospel songs her sister was playing. My grandmother was clapping, singing along to the gospel songs, and crying. I was afraid because I'd never heard her cry like this before. I thought to myself, "My dad must've been hurt pretty bad, but he's going to be alright."

The next day, we were back in Adel and preparing to go to the funeral. We were at my Grandmother Rosa's house. She had on a white dress, and everyone else had on black dresses and black suits. I still hadn't seen my daddy yet, and I was getting scared. Black limousines pulled up to her house, and the directors instructed us to get into the cars. As I looked around, everyone was crying and sad. I never shed a tear. I thought to myself, "Let's go, I'm ready to see my dad!"

The limousines took us right around the corner to the church. When we got into the church, I saw a box with an American flag on the top of it. As we were seated, people began to sing church songs, while others were crying loudly. I didn't know what my grandmother Virginia was doing because I wasn't sitting on the same row with her.

Then the Pastor over the service stood and said, "Next, we will have Lafayette Burns Jr. give a few words." This was the first time I saw his biological son. He was very sad as he spoke words of honor and appreciation for his father. After a few more songs, the Pastor came up and spoke. I was standing beside his grandson as he wept quietly. The Pastor delivered a message that would shape the way I viewed death.

He looked at me and my dad's grandson and told us, "Young men, don't cry. Lafayette is gone to Heaven to be with the Lord." I immediately looked up and smiled. I was happy. It warmed my heart to know that my dad had gone away to be with the one my grandmother talked about all the time.

During that moment, I evaluated whom my dad was with. The Lord is the reason we have a place to stay. He's the reason we have food on our table. He's the one that allowed me to be here today.

Two men in uniforms removed the flag from his casket and opened it. When they opened it, I saw him for the first time in three months. I was ready to go and see him, but I had to wait in line. When I finally got to see him, it looked as if he was asleep, but I remembered what the preacher said. He's gone to be with the Lord. I walked away, knowing I would see him tomorrow.

As the military men rolled him out of the sanctuary to load him in the car, I stood on the bottom step and watched. I started having flashbacks of watching JFK's funeral service on television and remembered when his son saluted him as he rode by. I looked around to make sure no one saw me and saluted him as they lifted him in the hearse.

At the cemetery, I saw more soldiers walking around in their uniforms. I was intrigued and curious because I didn't know what this meant. Suddenly, I heard gunshots! I was scared because it was the first time I'd heard a gun, besides watching westerns on television with my dad. I watched the soldiers take the flag off his box, fold the flag with precision, and give it to my grandmother Rosa.

A few months later, my grandmother Virginia and I were watching a television show about Dr. Martin Luther King. The show depicted the untimely and tragic end of his life.

"Momma, what happened to Martin Luther King?" I asked.

"He died, baby."

"Is that what happened to Daddy?" I asked her.

"Yes," she said in a low tone.

I immediately began to break down and cry because the television show made me realize that he was never coming back. I went and grabbed his picture off the shelf, sat in the rocking chair, held his picture to my heart, and cried. It was the first time I'd cried over the death of a loved one.

After I realized what death really meant, I began to fall into depression as an 8-year-old kid. I would cry in my room at night, thinking about my brothers and my dad. I thought feeling bad emotionally was the right thing to do every night because it felt right in my heart to cry.

After school, I would come home, do my chores, do my homework, watch Wheel of Fortune with my grandmother, and go to bed. I would go to bed and cry myself to sleep, thinking about my dad. I remember when I was a small boy lying in bed with my grandmother; she would talk to God every night before she went to bed. She would tell Him thank you for everything she could think of. I also thought back to what the preacher said in church. He stated that my dad was in heaven with the Lord.

I then began to talk to the Lord every night and tell Him thank you for everything that transpired in my day. The desire to see and talk to my dad again grew stronger as I got older, so I continued to talk to God every night before I went to bed.

At school, I would see kids being picked up by their parents and begin to think about my dad and become sad all over again. I would be standing in the bus line, ready to catch the bus home so that I wouldn't break down in front of the other kids.

My behavior at school was starting to take a turn for the worse. I would act out in school, play during class, and not listen to the teachers. I feared consequences, but my heart was so broken that I didn't care if I got into trouble. I would get pink slips for bad behavior, and my grandmother wouldn't spare the rod. I got many spankings for bad behavior and talking too much in class.

My grandmother told me, "If you get a negative on your report card for behavior, I'm going to whip your butt."

I already knew my report card was going to have a negative behavior report. I didn't want my grandmother to whip me, and I was really missing my dad. Before I went to catch the bus that morning, I reached into the cabinet, grabbed two rat poison pills, and put them into my jean jacket pocket. I thought to myself, "If I get a negative on my report card, I'm going to take these two pills so I can go and be with my dad."

Later that day, everyone was excited about their report cards as the teacher was handing them out. Once the teacher called my name, I went up to get my report card. I pulled it out of the brown envelope and saw the negative on my conduct. I thought to myself, "If I change the minus to a plus, I won't have to take the pills."

I sneaked into my book bag, got a pen, and changed the behavior to a plus. When I drew the cross over the minus to make it positive, the mark I made was red, and the original minus was black. There was no way that I could correct my mistake!

As the bell rang, I walked outside the classroom and went to the water fountain. I took the pills out of my pocket, swallowed them, and drank the water. I walked to my bus line and waited for my bus to come. I was waiting for the pills to take effect as all the other kids were excited about all the good grades they'd made. As I got on the bus, I was thinking to myself, "I'm still here."

As we pulled up to my neighborhood, my grandmother was in the yard waiting for me to get off the bus. She pulled out my report card, looked at it, and told me to get in the house and take my pants off. I got a spanking and a lesson for lying.

"If you tell one lie, you have to tell another one to cover up that lie," she said.

After the whipping, she made me take a bath and go to bed. I was happy that I didn't die from taking the pills.

CHAPTER 5
Appreciation in the Midst of Poverty

My grandmother was a hardworking woman. She made sure there was never a time that I hungered or didn't have any clean clothes to wear. My clothes may not have been name brand or even hand-me-downs, but they were clean, pressed, and presentable.

Every Saturday, my grandmother would have me bring my dirty clothes to the car porch so she could wash them in the washing machine outside. Once the clothes were done washing, she would gather them in a basket, take them behind the house, and hang them on the clothesline. She would take out her bag of wooden clothesline pins and begin the process.

"Pay attention," she said. "You're going to learn how to wash your own clothes and hang them on the line yourself."

She would write out a grocery list, provide me with food stamps, and send me to Bennett's Grocery. Mr. William Bennett, who was the owner of the grocery store, always made sure that I followed the instructions that my grandmother had given. He would always talk to me about being thankful to God and being obedient while I was away from my grandmother. Spice ham, bologna, souse meat, and ramen noodles were fast foods for me in the late '80s.

We began to fall on hard times, as my grandmother started having health issues. After years of throwing lumber around the yard at Del-Cook, she developed a tumor underneath her arm. This situation put her out of work for a while. There were times when the lights were turned off due to nonpayment.

I remember my grandmother praising God in the middle of the night while our lights were disconnected. All the windows of the house were open to keep the house cool throughout the night. Mosquitoes would come in and bite us up, but it really didn't matter to me. I was with my grandmother while she was praising God. Even though our lights were turned out, we still had running water and a roof over our heads. She would fix me breakfast with the meager food that we had in our home.

She would make me a bowl of government-provided cereal with water since we didn't have any milk. It was nasty at first, but I became accustomed to the taste and pretended it was milk. Regardless of the situation, I always made sure my grandmother knew how much I appreciated her.

At the age of 9, I learned to be thankful in every situation because things could've been worse. I was truly grateful because I thought about what would've happened if my grandmother hadn't chosen me out of my two brothers. Everything that my grandmother done for me was appreciated. I learned from my Uncle Fred the importance and power of appreciation, by the way he demonstrated it towards grandma. The more I appreciated my grandmother for the things she had done, it provided her with a sense of pride, knowing her sacrifice was not in vain.

With being out of work and my dad passing, my grandmother began to fall into depression. I recall my grandmother starting her day with a beer and continuing to drink throughout the day. I was happy because she was happy. I didn't understand the impact of alcohol and the issues it was causing in her body, but I knew it made her happy. That's all I ever wanted—for her to be happy.

My grandmother listened to a lot of gospel and blues with her friends. She listened to a particular song called "Members Only" by Bobby Blue Bland. The song talked about how if you were broken, you could be a part of this party. You didn't need a checkbook; just bring your broken heart. My grandmother and all her friends were truly broken by the things that happened over the years in their lives. I watched my grandmother drink every day with her friends, as they enjoyed being around each other.

At night, when her friends would leave, things would always take a turn for the worse. My grandmother would be in the bathroom throwing up. I was scared because I'd never heard her be in so much pain. She would be in the bathroom for extended periods of time, regurgitating all the alcohol she drank during the day. Afterwards, she would shower and go to bed. This took place every night.

I remember going to school and thinking about the pain my grandmother was in the night before. While I was in class, I could hear the sounds of her pain in my heart. School became a place of escape for me because it allowed me to put my mind on new and fresh things.

On the weekends, her niece, Sandra from Quitman, would come into town and bring her son, LeVert, with her. He was the tallest kid I've ever seen in my life. I thought to myself, "Here's another opportunity for me to make a new friend." Boy, was I wrong! My cousin turned out to be the one that God would use to teach me a hard lesson. You can't be a weakling because of your circumstances.

When we played with each other, he always took the opportunity to pick me up and power-drive me to the ground. If we were playing football in the front yard, he didn't stop until I was in the bushes. He was bigger and stronger than I was.

One day, my grandmother saw us in the yard playing. She caught him in action as he picked me up and threw me in the ditch. I got up and started crying.

She said, "Stop all that crying and learn how to be tough."

That threw me for a loop because I thought that my grandmother would always protect me from any situation that would bring me harm. Once we were done playing, we would become friends as if he never threw me in the woods.

I knew my grandmother would be drinking, so I would ask her if I could go to Quitman and stay with my cousins for the weekend. When my grandmother said yes, my cousin and I would both run to my room. He would help me get some clothes to stay with them for the weekend. Once we got in the car and drove off, I would stare into the night sky and look at the stars through the back window. I was thankful for the opportunity to get away.

Seeing and hearing my grandmother in pain daily was taking a toll on me. When we got to their house, I saw things that I never knew existed. My Cousin Levert asked, "Momma, can we play the Nintendo?"

"Yes, but you will not be up all night," she said.

When he turned on the television, I saw the words "Mario Brothers."

"Here, Chip, you take this controller," he said.

I didn't know what was going on. I saw a man jumping and running on television. It looked as if he was controlling this man with what he had in his hands. It was so fun to see, and I couldn't wait for my turn. When it was my time to play, I would only last for 4 seconds because I didn't know the concept of this game or what I was supposed to do. LeVert would show me how to play the game, and once I learned it, I became good at it.

"That's enough," Aunt Sandra said. "Y'all turn that game off and get in the bed," she said.

The next day, she would wake us up for breakfast.

"Momma, can we have some white spaghetti?" LeVert asked.

I thought to myself, "What is that?"

Once she finished preparing it, she had us sit down and enjoy the meal. It was Ramen noodles with sausages diced up in it. It was delicious! Once we were done, we would go outside and jump on the trampoline. This was my first experience of jumping on anything like this. And that's when the wrestling began again! My cousin performed every wrestling move he saw on TV on me. I had to learn how to defend myself quickly. There were no adults around, and no one was going to bail me out of this challenge. Once he saw that I wouldn't back down from the challenge, we became more and more like brothers.

My Aunt Sandra had me come into the house and try on some old clothes that LeVert couldn't wear anymore. She gave me shoes, shirts, and pants that fit me perfectly. On Sundays, she would get us dressed for church and have us walk there. The church was only a minute away from her house. I saw children my age singing in the choir and older children leading songs. I've never seen anything like this, and it intrigued me.

After church, we'd head back to Adel. I was happy to go back, but I didn't want to leave. Being away was a relief from witnessing my grandmother's struggle with pain and depression. The journey back for me meant facing the reality that my grandmother was not healthy. Once I got home, I told my grandmother about the time I had and showed her the clothes that I received from my aunt.

The next day at school, I felt like a new kid because of the clothes that were gifted to me. Even though they were hand-me-downs, I was appreciative of them.

Things changed drastically within a year. My dad died, my grandmother was out of work, and Christmas was approaching. The Christmas tree that was normally in the front room by the door was no longer there. It was replaced with a small tree sitting on the stand in the corner of the living room. In the past, my grandmother would have gifts under the tree the night before. I remember getting up in the middle of the night and tearing small holes in presents to see what they were.

The next morning, I got up and rushed to the small tree, hoping that there would be gifts. The tree was empty, and I immediately looked at my grandmother. She was in the kitchen leaning over the sink and cleaning chitlings. I could tell she was sad.

"Merry Christmas, Chip," she said in a low tone.

"What's wrong, Momma?" I asked.

"I feel so bad that I wasn't able to get you anything this year, baby," she said.

I told her, "I'm thankful to be here with you, and the food you're cooking is good enough for me." She looked at me and smiled. I ran to her and gave her a hug. She immediately changed her countenance, and her spirits were lifted.

She had a small radio on top of the deep freezer. She turned on the gospel music and began to praise the Lord and cook with so much joy. When she was happy, I was happy. I stood at the door and saw my friends riding their new bicycles and wearing their new outfits. Inside, I was sad that I couldn't get anything, but I never let my grandmother see my disappointment.

Each day, my heart was filled with appreciation for her preventing me from being adopted. Nothing in this world could ever amount to the gift of her choosing me.

CHAPTER 6
I Can't Go for That

My Uncle Fred, who is my grandmother Virginia's son, was a giant in my eyes as a kid. He always worked out in the backyard, did push-ups daily, and ate very little. He dropped out of school and became a mechanic at Hazel's Garage, which was the premier mechanic shop in Adel. Even though he dropped out of school, he was still doing something productive to make a living.

One of the main lessons I learned from my uncle is to be appreciative of your mother and never take her for granted. After every meal, he would say, "Momma, the food was good, and I appreciate the meal." He would walk into the house after he came home from work, kiss her on the jaw, and put money in her hand every time he got paid. I said to myself, "When I grow up, I want to be able to give my grandmother some money, too!"

I spent a lot of time with my uncle. He would take me riding with him in his all-white Nova with the black rally stripes. This was a race car he built with his own hands. It was fast and very loud!

On Saturdays, he would park the car under the porch to give it a wash. He would play music that I'd never heard before, which shaped and influenced me early in my life. I wanted to be just like him. At night, I would grab a clothing hanger out of the closet, sit on the edge of my bed, and use the hanger as a steering wheel. I would pretend that the hanger was a steering wheel and drive all over the world in my mind. My imagination made up the difference for the toys I didn't have physically as a child.

My uncle would always have a lot of friends over in Momma's backyard. They were drinking, smoking, and socializing all day long. At this point in my life, I knew it wasn't the right thing to do. I learned from watching educational programs on Georgia Public Television to say no to drugs and how they affected our lives.

Some days, I would go outside and see people smoking out of soda cans. I didn't know what it was, but it didn't seem right. One day, I ran behind the house, and I saw my uncle using the can, which he immediately dropped. He told me, "Chip, what I'm doing is not the right thing to do. Don't you ever do this, nephew. Now go and play."

"Yes Sir," I said as I ran off.

There would be times when I would see my uncle reading the Bible and working out in his room. Then, the next minute, the room would be engulfed with smoke, which was different from cigarette smoke. It made him act in a way that made me fear him. I made sure to stay close to my grandmother because I didn't like to see him that way. Even when my uncle used drugs, he made sure that I never saw him do it. He was battling to stay away from using drugs, but the environment was not helping him win at all.

I remember him checking himself into Greenleaf so many times to get help. I missed my uncle while he was gone. He needed God, but he was too distracted with the women and the cars to focus on being delivered from his addiction, which grew over time. I never judged my uncle. Even in his lowest moments, I always looked up to him and remembered what he told me: "Don't you ever do this!"

One night, my mother, Ladedra, came by the house. I was so excited to see her. I ran to her and gave her a hug. Despite leaving me with my grandmother, my love for her never changed as a child. She went into the back room and began talking with my grandmother. I heard their voices escalate, as it sounded like they were having an argument. I sat on the couch and watched television to drown out what they were saying.

They finally came out of the room and continued to argue as my mother prepared to leave.

"Where are those two boys at, Ladedra?" my grandmother asked.

"I don't know where they are, and I don't care if they are living or dead," my mother replied as she walked out of the house and slammed the door.

It broke my heart to hear her say those words because I missed them so much. I got up from the couch I was sitting on and sat down in the corner of the living room. I was so hurt that I just wanted to be alone.

"Chip, you want to come into the room and watch television with me?" my grandmother asked.

"No, ma'am, I'm just going to sit here for a while," I replied.

As she closed her bedroom door, I was sitting alone in the corner. I began to cry so much. I sat still and comprehended what she said. The more I understood what that meant, the more the tears flowed out of my eyes and down my face. I cried myself to sleep in the corner.

The next morning, I woke up to my grandmother standing over me.

"Chip, everything will be alright," she said. "Get up and get ready for breakfast," she said.

As I walked to the bathroom, the tears began to flow again because I remembered what my mother said the night before.

CHAPTER 7
Close Your Eyes and Make Believe

1990 continued to be a tough year for my grandmother and me. She was still out of work, and I was getting older. Her drinking got worse, and so did her depression. No one knew she was depressed but me. When everyone was around, she would have that golden smile on her face and be so full of joy. But when everyone left, she would be in so much pain, not only in her body, but also in her soul.

She'd lost so much weight from drinking, but I didn't perceive anything to be wrong. She was superwoman in my eyes, and there was no way that she could be affected negatively by any situation. As I began to grow older, she grew older as well. Her patience with me was not the way it was years ago.

My grandmother's niece and her children from Daytona Beach, Florida, came and visited us in the summer of 1990. My cousin, Leroy, instantly took a liking to me. He was very outgoing and had a lot of money! I mean, a lot of money!

My cousin, Leroy, asked if I could come and spend the summer with them in Daytona.

"Please, Momma, can I go?" I asked.

"Edith, if it's okay with you, he can go," my grandmother replied.

She said yes, and I sprinted to my room to pack my clothes for the summer. I didn't know I was preparing to have the best time of my life! The trip there reminded me of the times when I would ride with my grandmother on long trips. Once I arrived, I was introduced to family members I had never met before.

The next day, my cousin enrolled me in a summer program for the youth at Bethune Cookman College. Every day, we took trips all over Florida. I experienced swimming in a pool that made automatic waves. My cousin Leroy trained me to drive a speed boat in the middle of the Atlantic Ocean. We would drive far out to the marshes and park. He took out meat from the boat and placed it on the edge of the marsh. Within minutes, he would fill multiple buckets with fish.

When I watched the Andy Griffith show, I would see him fishing with a pole. I'd never seen someone fish with just a net, but it worked. Every day, after every adventure, my cousins took me to Checkers. I would order whatever I wanted with no limit. This was the first time in my life that there was no limit to anything I desired. This was different from my life back at home in Georgia.

Every day, I looked forward to going to the beach. Being around the ocean gave me a peace that I never knew I needed as a child. Daily, I stood at the shore and smelled the ocean air as all the pain in my heart melted away. My cousins treated me so kindly in Florida. I felt special there, despite feeling like I was not worthy of being a son to my biological parents.

This trip eased my mind and taught me that I must be very special to God. I began to think about everything I had experienced in my life and concluded that it wasn't my fault and everything would work out fine for me. The more I hung around other kids from different nationalities and different backgrounds, the more confident and outgoing I became.

One day, while we were at a pool, I noticed kids doing backflips in the water in the 5-foot area. I was intrigued by it and decided to give it a try. Every attempt I made was unsuccessful, and the kids laughed at me. I decided to walk around the pool and sit at the edge until everyone left. Once I had the pool to myself, I began to practice doing backflips in the pool. I was determined that I wouldn't let anyone laugh at me without redeeming myself.

In an empty pool, I stood and jumped backward into the pool. Suddenly, I got stuck upside down in the water. I lost my sense of direction regarding what was up and what was down. I was drowning, and no one was there to help me. I fought to get to the top of the water, but time was running out. Finally, I made it back to the top! I immediately got out of the pool and never attempted that move again in my life!

As I began my 5th-grade year back in Georgia, I grew weary of being in the house with my grandmother during those depressing times. There were occasions when I began to grow disobedient to what my grandmother was instructing me to do. The pressure of raising a young adolescent child, being laid off from work, dealing with a tumor in her stomach, and alcoholism began to get the best of my grandmother.

One day, I made my grandmother very upset by not listening to her, so she decided that it was best for me to go and live with my aunt. I told her that I didn't want to leave, but she made me pack my things. I went into the room she blessed me to live in for 10 years and packed every item I had. It hurt me so deeply because I never wanted to leave my grandmother's side. Looking back at it today, it was the best decision at the time because my grandmother was not the best version of herself.

I asked her if I could have another chance to stay.

"No, Chip! You're getting too grown, and you need to be with your aunt. You don't even feel these butt whippings anymore."

She was right about that.

I moved in with my aunt and her husband. My life took on a whole new meaning. My uncle was a very unselfish man. He loved me like I was his son. He was a truck driver, just like my dad, Lafayette, was. He would take me all over the South and talk to me about getting older. He was a Cowboys fanatic! I didn't know what football was until I met him. He told me all the stories he had experienced playing football in high school. I began to become interested in sports because of his influence.

My aunt was very strict with me because of the disobedience at my grandmother's house. One thing my aunt always did was make sure that I had the best of everything. She made sure that I studied, did my chores, and taught me how to carry myself as a young man. She taught me the importance of grooming and being always presentable in public. She always took me shopping to buy me the most up-to-date clothes.

With all these blessings, I was still missing being with my grandmother. My mind was on her all the time, and I was sorry for disappointing her. One day, my grandmother informed us that my mother had a daughter and left her at home alone in Tampa, Florida. My grandmother and her sister went to pick her up. They returned with a little girl.

"What's her name, Momma?" I asked.

"Her name is Lesha. This is your sister," my grandmother said.

I stared at her, and she stared at me while sucking her two middle fingers. My sister and I became close instantly.

Every Sunday, my aunt would take us to Holy Community Church. We attended Sunday service regularly. The more we attended, the more I began to pay attention to the Pastor of the Church, Rev. Horne. He was different from any man I've ever seen in my life. He was a man of morals and believed that the word of God could turn anyone's life around.

When I became a member of his church, my life as a young child took off. I went from being average in school to making all A's. I learned early on that God can heal my broken heart and make me whole in my mind so that I can learn. The more I listened to his teachings on Sunday, the more it influenced me to be a better young person in the classroom and a better child at home.

CHAPTER 8
The Power of Worship

My aunt had four young daughters, including my sister and I, as she also took on the responsibility of raising us as well. There was a total of six children under one roof. There was no bed for me. I had to make a pallet on the floor to sleep at night. Every morning, I would wake up, fold my brown blanket, and place it on the shelf in the laundry area. My aunt was very particular about placing things where they belonged.

My uncle was a truck driver, and my aunt was a supervisor at Captain D's. This left me with the responsibility of taking care of the girls once I got out of school. I would ensure their homework was done, make sure they were fed, and keep them safe until my aunt came home from work. I didn't live the normal life of a young 11-year-old boy. I started to understand that I was the nephew and not the son. Even though my aunt and uncle loved me like their own, in my heart, I desired to be with my mother and father, too.

I remember when Rev. Horne would preach about praising God. There was one song he would always sing. It was titled *Worship Him.* In the song, the lyrics were, "Let's forget about ourselves, concentrate on Him, and worship Him." The way he would sing that song in church before he preached really inspired me. At night, I would praise God while lying on the floor and thank Him for all He has done for me. Even though I was sleeping on the floor, I had a place to stay. Even though my grandmother put me out, she put me in a better situation to be raised by adults I couldn't get over on. I was thankful.

Music became a part of my healing and my gateway to escape the wounds that my soul encountered in my young life. One Sunday morning, I was watching B.E.T. before church. There was a gospel video that came on and grabbed my attention right away. The song was called *Optimistic* by Sounds of Blackness. This song spoke to every challenge I've experienced in my life. The lyrics were, "As long as you keep your head to the sky, you can win." This song lifted me in my heart. As I comprehended what the words were saying, the tears immediately began to flow. I was broken through all the experiences in my life thus far, but I was encouraged to keep my head up.

My self-esteem was very low. At times, I would think about how much of a failure I was for disappointing my grandmother and her not wanting me to live with her anymore.

One morning, I missed the bus to school. It was my fault for waking up late. I asked my aunt to take me to school.

"No," she replied. "You will walk to school. Since you slept in late, walk!"

"Yes ma'am," I said. I grabbed my book bag and headed out the door.

The school was nearly three miles away. I chose to walk the back route to school because I needed to encourage myself privately. Once I got on the dirt road where no one could see me, I started singing, "As long as you keep your head to the sky, you can win." It played over and over in my head. Even though I was encouraged, cool tears were flowing from my eyes. I didn't care how I looked because I was on the dirt road, and no one could see me.

Being that this was my 5th grade year, things began to come together for me in my learning. This was the first time that I made all A's consecutively. I was doing so well academically that my aunt and uncle afforded me the opportunity to play recreation football. I was excited about my first time being on a sports team. The team consisted of 5th and 6th graders who had played the game for years.

Our coach made us do running drills and conditioning on the first day of practice. I thought to myself, "This is not as hard as I thought." The next day's practice consisted of tackling drills.

Coach Ramone, our head coach, stated, "It's time to hit today!"

Everybody was excited, but I was scared! My first time being hit in a tackling drill really made me consider quitting the team and going back home to play video games after school. After those first few hits, my fear of facing challenges dissipated. We went 8-0 our first year and won the championship, and I never played a down in the game.

"Next year, you will be ready, Chip, but now is not your time," Coach Ramone said. He taught me the importance of celebrating others and preparing for your opportunity while you wait.

The next year, most of the players were promoted to the 7th grade, which left a few of us returning for the next season. I went from being on the bench to being the starting quarterback. Needless to say, I wasn't the best at the position, as we lost every game. To start off going 8-0 and then going 0-8 taught me that nothing in life will be given to you. If you inherit greatness, you must work even harder to keep it.

Once I completed practice during the week, I had the responsibility of coming home and doing chores as a 6th grader. My aunt would always give me set chores that had to be completed before she got home. One day, I was so hungry that I made myself a bowl of cereal when I came home from school.

When my aunt got home, she asked, "Chip, did you have cereal?"

"No, ma'am," I replied. I wasn't telling the truth. She noticed that I had dropped cereal on the floor and didn't clean up behind myself.

"Are you sure you didn't eat any cereal?" she asked again.

"No, I didn't," I replied.

"Come here and open your mouth," she said.

She looked in my mouth and saw that I had eaten cereal and lied to her. She took off her belt and immediately began to whip me for lying to her. I tried to get away from her whipping me and ended up damaging her kitchen wall, leaving a hole in it.

"That's it! Go and pack your clothes. I'm taking you back to Momma's house," she said.

I went to the room, fell on my knees, and began to cry as I started packing all my shoes out of the closet. I felt so bad that I lied to her. I began to think to myself that nobody wanted me. I started thinking to myself that I wished I was adopted, too. I didn't know how to feel. All I remember is that I was tired of crying and hurting in my heart. I was tired of thinking about all the negative experiences that had taken place in my life.

I wanted to live a normal life like my friends and be happy. I packed all my belongings in two large trash bags, loaded them up in the truck, and she took me back to my grandmother's house. My grandmother was glad to have me back, and I was happy to be back home. I went from sleeping on the floor to having my own bedroom again. It's amazing how you don't realize what you have until it's gone.

Thanks be to God that even in my disobedience as an adolescent, He allowed me to come back and prove that I could be better. Even though I made mistakes living with my aunt, I learned how to be more responsible and get things done without someone telling me to do them.

I knew about accountability, as Grandmother Rosa taught me to always do the right things. The challenge was knowing how to do what was right when no one was watching me.

CHAPTER 9
There's No Place Like Home

In 1995, I developed a strong desire to see my biological father again. After all those years that had gone by without seeing him, I still had questions about my father. Over the years, I would always ask my grandmother where my father lived. One day, I asked her, and she made it very clear she'd grown tired of me asking.

"He's in Hickory, North Carolina, Chip! Now, don't ask me that no more!" she said.

In school, we learned about 411, a service provided by AT&T that would give you a phone number if you provided a name, city, and state. I was hesitant to dial it, but I decided to give it a try. I dialed 411 and provided my father's name, city, and state. Immediately, the operator gave me a phone number!

"Would you like for me to connect you?" the operator asked.

"Yes," I replied as my heart began to race. The phone rang twice, and suddenly, a man with a deep voice answered the phone.

"Hello," he answered.

"Hello, is this Walter Richards?" I replied.

"Yes," he answered.

I replied, "This is your son, Eric Richards."

We were both shocked. He was shocked that I found him, and I was shocked that he knew who I was. As I was talking with him, my aunt and cousins were amazed that I found my dad.

"I want to come pick you up for the summer and spend some time with you," he said.

He and my aunt talked on the phone about the plan, and they agreed that he could come and pick me up for the summer. It was one of the best days of my life! After all those years of asking my grandmother where he was, I finally found my biological father. I'm so glad she remembered his name and where he was from.

As the day approached, he came to pick me up, and I thought about how much fun I was going to have. I thought about the excitement of going to a whole new state. I remember rehearsing how I was going to call him Dad. Suddenly, there was a heavy knock at the door. I ran to the door and asked, "Who is it?"

"Walter," he replied.

As I opened the door, it was as if time stood still. I couldn't move. I embraced the moment of seeing him for the first time in 15 years. He grabbed me and gave me a strong bear hug. I felt his disappointment and shame as he embraced me. As we greeted each other, my aunt, grandmother, sister, and cousins were all in tears and smiles. I was nervous talking to my father for the first time, but things began to flow naturally.

My grandmother instructed him to bring me back to Georgia before the new school year started. As we began the journey to North Carolina, I started thinking about all the times that I asked my grandmother where he was. And now, I was in the car with him. It was as if I manifested my desire by using the tools around me to bring it to pass.

As we entered North Carolina, I saw mountains for the first time. I was taking in the scenery of something new and intriguing that I'd never seen before. Once we arrived, my dad took me to meet his mother. She was so excited to see me. I was amazed to see someone other than my family back home who resembled me.

"Momma, this is Eric, my son from Georgia," my dad said.

"I know who he is."

"What's your name, Grandma?" I asked.

"You can call me Mother Abraham," she said. "Now tell me, what do you like to eat?"

"I like fish, cheese grits, and hush puppies. My grandmother back at home makes that for me sometimes," I replied.

She gave my dad some money to go grocery shopping for me and gave me some money to play games at the store. She was very nice to me. One day, she took me with her to the church she attended. She made me sit as she took out cleaning items and started cleaning the church. She was singing gospel songs and wiping down the pews. As I was sitting in the church, I began to thank God that I finally found my dad.

Every day while I was there, he would take me to my grandmother's house, and I would be with her while he worked. I asked him if I could go to work with him one day because I wanted to spend some time with him. He agreed and took me with him to work. He was a janitor at a local high school.

"I used to be pretty good at playing basketball until I hurt my knee," he said.

He showed me pictures of himself inside the case at the school and his name on the wall inside the gym. Seeing this gave me confidence that I had what it takes to be a better athlete. I remember doing football drills on the Hickory High School football field by myself. Something was happening in my mind. I wanted to come and live with my father after spending one week with him.

I called home and asked my grandmother if I could come and live with my dad.

"No, Chip. You've been in Adel for fifteen years. You're not going to move to North Carolina after one trip. I know you're having fun being around your dad, but we're going to finish what we started," my grandmother said.

I wasn't sad about her decision. I wanted to know what it was like to live my life with my father raising me. Day after day, my dad would take me to Grandmother Abraham's house while I was there. She would read me scriptures and educate me on who my grandfather was and my dad's life growing up.

"Your grandmother has done a wonderful job raising you. You're very respectful and mannerable. If you continue to be that way, you will go far in life," she said.

I became attached to her while I was there. Instead of connecting with my dad, I grew a bond with my Grandmother Abraham. As time was winding down, I knew it was time for me to prepare to get back home to Georgia. She took me to the church one last time to help her clean and sweep the sanctuary. She was a servant. She loved serving. She taught me about the Richards' family tree, shared her wisdom with me, and showed me how to be a servant while no one was watching. Everything she shared with me was identical to the same lessons instilled in me back at home.

"Walter, it's time to take Eric back to Georgia. He must be in school next week," my Grandmother Abraham said.

"I can't take him back until next week," my dad replied.

My dad couldn't keep his promise to have me back at the agreed-upon time.

"Son, I can't take you back to Georgia, so you must catch the Greyhound bus home," he said.

I was scared because I had never been on a Greyhound before and was only fifteen years old.

I said, "I want you to take me back, Dad; I don't want to ride the bus home."

"I have no choice, son; you have to ride the bus back home," he said.

I called home to tell my grandmother Virginia about the change of plans, and she was furious. Nevertheless, she gave me specific instructions on how to conduct myself on the bus.

"Do the right thing, pay attention to your surroundings, and keep your mouth closed," she said.

I gave my Grandmother Abraham a long hug, as she told me she loved me.

"Call me when you get home, Eric. I will be waiting for your call," she said.

The next morning at 4:00 a.m., my dad dropped me off at the Greyhound station with two tickets. He gave me instructions on when I was supposed to switch over to another bus in South Carolina.

"You're going to be on the bus for 13 hours, but you will be fine," he said.

I was ready to get back to Georgia.

'How could my dad send me back to Georgia like this?' I thought to myself.

I ran to a seat in the back of the bus and sat by myself. I was watching everyone and making sure that no one was out to get me. After a couple of hours into the trip, I became more relaxed and settled, but I didn't go to sleep. I came to grips with the fact that this was the only way I was getting home, and I must grow up right now!

I didn't have any food to eat or any money. All I had were my instructions from my grandmother Virginia: "Do the right thing, pay attention to your surroundings, and keep your mouth closed!" On the way home, I began to reminisce about my experience in North Carolina. I thought about how excited I was to see my dad, but also about the fact that he didn't bring me back to Georgia. I was disappointed and sorry that I considered wanting to leave my family in Georgia to be with my dad.

After fourteen long hours, I finally made it home. My aunt was at the bus station to pick me up. I was happy to see her and told her about my experience. My aunt allowed me to use her car phone to call my dad and grandmother to let them know I arrived. Once I got home to my grandmother's house, she explained to me that you can't make life decisions about someone the first time you meet them. I thought about the phone call I had with her while I was in North Carolina. I was glad that I finally got the opportunity to meet my dad after fifteen years, but there's no place like home.

CHAPTER 10
Time is Winding Down

It was the fall of 1995, and it was time to begin my freshman year in high school. This was the moment I always dreamed of as a kid. There was only one issue: I didn't have any new school clothes. I didn't ask my grandmother if she could buy me any clothes because she wasn't working. I needed some school clothes and was willing to do anything to get them. It was at that moment that I made a conscious decision to go against how I was raised and do the wrong thing.

In my neighborhood, the sale of narcotics was a constant occurrence. One of my older friends was always around the action. I approached him and inquired about selling drugs.

"Why do you want to do this?" he asked.

"I need some school clothes, and I don't have any money," I replied.

"I will not give you anything, nor will anybody around here give you anything to sell," he replied. "I'm going to tell everybody around here not to entertain you if you ask them. If you come and ask me or anybody else again, I'm going to tell Mrs. Virginia about you," he said. "You're going to be a great football player one day. You're 15 years old, and we will not allow you to destroy your life for some clothes. Now get out of my face," he said.

I walked away, ashamed and thankful at the same time. I never wanted to enter that type of lifestyle, but it was the easiest way to change my situation, considering I couldn't get a job without a social security number. If it wasn't for my friend redirecting me to focus on another path, I don't know where I would be today.

My first day of school was a very humbling one. I was in class with everyone who had new clothes on, while I had the same clothes from the last two years. I had to learn how to be confident in who I was and not what I was wearing. During lunch, all the football players would sit at the same table and joke with each other. I was the laughingstock. I had to learn how to stand up for myself and dish out jokes instead of just taking them. No one in high school cared about the hard life I lived. There was no time to explain my situation.

As I began to matriculate through school, I became a comedian outside the classroom. I refused to let people laugh at the poverty that I was wearing.

As I entered the summer of my sophomore year, I was determined to get a job, even though I didn't have a social security number. I walked across the bridge to the King Frog Shopping Plaza in Adel and went from store to store to ask for a summer job. I didn't have a resume or a social security number. All I had was my word that I would do a good job. Every store I went to turned me away. I was told no so many times that I would go behind the plaza and cry. I was trying to be like the other teenagers and get a summer job to make some extra cash the right way, but I didn't have a social security number.

I was discouraged, but I didn't stop. I would dry my face, walk to other stores, and try again. I walked into another restaurant and asked to speak to the manager.

"Hello, young man. How can I help you?" she asked.

I told her my situation, and she didn't flinch. She kept a straight face and told me to have a seat in the lobby. She made a phone call and got it approved for me to get paid under the table. I didn't know what that meant at the time, but she explained the conditions, and I accepted. She gave me a uniform with a hat and my name tag! I was excited and couldn't wait to tell my grandmother that I got a job.

Once she gave me all my items and told me when to report back to work, I rushed home and told my grandmother about the good news! My grandmother was so happy and proud that I got a job despite all the rejection from other companies. I would work from 8:00 in the morning till 12:00 at night with no problem. Every payday, I received cash instead of a check. It didn't matter to me. I was happy that I could buy what I needed and help my grandmother with the needs around the house.

Once football practice began in the summer, I had to leave the job. I didn't have to give a two-week notice because it was already determined what day I would have to stop working. I really appreciated the store manager for giving me the opportunity when everyone else turned me down.

Sports became a major part of my life in high school. Not only did sports become a way of life, but it also became therapeutic for me. On the football field, I could channel my life's frustrations and release them while playing the game. My junior year was very formidable. I was the starting fullback and middle linebacker. I wasn't the best on the field, but I played the game with passion and violence. Every snap was an opportunity to move towards my goal of being a professional football player.

Every time I put on the helmet, I thought about all the times my grandmother sacrificed for me. I thought about my brothers being given up for adoption. I thought about my dad, Lafayette. I thought about how neither of my parents was around to see me mature and evolve. High school football allowed me to put into practice everything I learned as a kid. It afforded me the opportunity to show what

I was capable of. All the bad breaks, disappointments, and anger were released on Friday nights.

The Lord always placed someone around me who was in a better situation than I was, to show me that nothing is impossible. His name is James Payne. He was the total opposite of who I was in life. He was fast, well-dressed, smart, and fortunate enough to have both of his parents present in his life. He also had transportation every year we were in high school. He would come and pick me up for school every morning. He was a real friend. He embodied everything my Grandmother Rosa instilled in me: Always do the right thing while no one is watching you.

In the classroom, he excelled. In the weight room, he didn't skip reps. On the field, he was a champion. He was a brother to me. He didn't judge my situation or look down on how I was brought up. He embraced me as a brother. He would get letters and visits from colleges all over the country. Whenever he talked about colleges visiting him and his success stories, it filled me with hope that I, too, could achieve that same success. Our brotherhood showed me that it's okay to be happy for your friends. Sometimes, the people closest to you will be the main ones that despise your success.

As I made it to my senior year, I became the captain of the football team and was elected President of the Fellowship of Christian Athletes. Despite missing a year of school and facing numerous challenges growing up, I matured quickly and was able to translate my faith into character and action.

One Friday afternoon, as we were loading the bus for a road game, my coach asked me about my birth records.

"Chip, will you have your birth certificate before you graduate?" my coach asked.

"Yeah, Coach, we're working on it." I replied. I wasn't confident that we were going to have my birth certificate by graduation time. Consistently, we would contact the White House and the U.S. Embassy about my records and never get a response. Time was running out. My coach informed me that schools were coming to visit me, but they couldn't make any offers because I didn't have a social security number.

My story began to spread around the region. City officials and local news stations would come and visit me at school to learn about my story. One day, while I was sitting in class, my teacher received instructions from the intercom to send me to the office. I was nervous, as I didn't know what to expect. When I got to the office, I was met by a team from the *Tifton Gazette News* to interview me about my story. I explained to them my situation and the years my family reached out to the government to obtain a copy of my birth certificate.

Even though things were looking as if I wouldn't obtain my records, I still had hope. I always thought that I would be able to make it through life without my birth records, but that was only in my hometown. Without proof of birth, I couldn't prove I was a citizen, become eligible to receive scholarships, or join the military. It was a miracle that I made it this far without a birth certificate.

The blunder that was made in my youth at the hands of someone else was beginning to manifest itself as a major roadblock in my life.

The editor of *Tifton Gazette News* asked the school administration if it was possible to take a picture of me standing over the bridge of I-75. The administration consented. This article ended up making the front page of the news, and quickly, the word began to spread about my case around the state.

The next week, during basketball practice, my friends and teammates saw the article and were joking about the situation.

"Chip, you're an illegal alien! How can you be in school with no social security number?" They would ask jokingly.

I played it off and laughed along with them, but deep down inside, I was embarrassed and ashamed. They never experienced the days I had to walk to work when I was a child because my grandmother couldn't find a babysitter. They never knew about the days I used to sit at home and dream of being a student in kindergarten. While everyone was joking about my story, I couldn't hold it against them. As a senior and a captain of the varsity basketball team, I quickly had to mature and recognize that my teammates wouldn't be able to understand the pain that I was dealing with, and it wasn't their fault. I just laughed along with them and kept my faith in God.

One day, when I got home from school, my grandmother greeted me with a smile and some good news!

"Chip, I got a phone call from Sanford Bishop's office today! Sanford Bishop is going to help us with our case," she said.

I was full of joy to know that God had intervened and provided us hope through a well-known congressman. Even though I was excited, I was still facing the reality of the unknown. If my birth certificate didn't arrive before next fall, I wouldn't be able to graduate high school, attend college, gain employment, obtain a driver's license, or join the military.

The spring of 2000 came around, and I still hadn't received my birth certificate. The days began to become shorter, as graduation day was rapidly approaching. Every day I woke up, I would think to myself, 'This could be the day my birth certificate comes in the mail.' Day after day, I would ask my grandmother if any mail came, and her answer would be no.

Then, suddenly, what seemed impossible and unattainable came forth. We received a copy of my birth certificate a month before my graduation day! I remember opening the mail and seeing my name, my parents' signatures, my birthdate, and the hospital where I was born. I cried tears of joy as I held on to something that was invisible in my life for 19 years. I was now able to prove citizenship, attend college, gain employment, obtain a driver's license, or even join the military if I so desired.

There was only one catch to the discovery of my birth records. My birthday was listed as November 26, while we celebrated my birthday on November 28.

"We have been celebrating your birthday on the wrong day for 18 years!" my grandmother said.

We both laughed about our newfound discovery but continued to praise God that I was finally able to move forward in life with proof of citizenship. After years of praying and keeping the faith, I went on to graduate and receive my high school diploma. Graduation was full of excitement and triumph for me. It was also a moment of joy for everyone who played a part in helping me reach this beautiful chapter in my life. All I could do was rejoice and smile because I never thought I would see this day.

My grandmother never gave up on me having a normal life as a child. She went through every wall that was before me and tore it down with optimism and the belief that God had a plan and purpose for my life. Because of the persistence of my grandmother, I experienced a victory that seemed impossible.

Immediately after graduation, I applied to attend college at Albany State University. I had dreams and aspirations of becoming a teacher and a high school basketball coach while pursuing a collegiate football career that could possibly land me in the NFL. I was accepted into college a few weeks later after applying. I was so thankful that I made it through all those years of struggle, sacrifice, and uncertainty. Finally, I reached a turning point where I could aspire for more.

It was my last Saturday in my bedroom as a newly accepted freshman in college. As I began to pack all my clothes and box up everything in my room that I would need for college, I began to think back to the first time I came to my grandmother's house back in the '80s. I remember how my grandmother chose me out of my two brothers. I began to think back on how my grandmother didn't know how she was going to make ends meet at times. I took a moment just to reflect and thank God for all the times he made a way out of no way for us.

Many thoughts began to race through my mind as I was preparing to enter the next stage of my life. After I finished packing all my things and preparing to lie down one more night in my room, I remember telling myself that I have an obligation to show my grandmother how appreciative I am for what she did for me. I was determined to be somebody. I was determined that I would not fail. I was determined that all her sacrifices for me were not in vain.

The next day, my aunt came to pick me up. As I loaded the truck with all my belongings, I promised my grandmother that one day, I would show her how much I appreciated all the sacrifices she made for me. As we drove off from the home that God blessed me to live, grow, and become, I left with a charge that it was time to put into action all the things I was taught. Despite all the challenges, I was thankful that I graduated from high school, but I knew this was just the beginning.

CHAPTER 11
Grace and Favor

My first year of college was filled with a lot of challenges. I wasn't the smartest, but I was dedicated to passing my classes. I didn't receive any scholarships, nor did my family have a college trust fund set up for me. Every dollar I used to attend college came from Pell Grants and student loans. I would take out thousands of dollars to attend college, not realizing that I would have to pay this money back one day. I took the loans with the expectation that I would graduate from college and make enough money to pay it all back and have enough to live a great life.

My first year of matriculation didn't even count toward my graduation. I was enrolled in developmental studies for one year before I could even enter college courses that would count towards my graduation. As I began to navigate college life, I was in a city by myself with no family and no one standing over my shoulder, making me study or go to class. There was one thing that held me accountable every day that I woke up: I must graduate to defeat the odds. I didn't want to come this far only to flunk out of school and go back home a failure. That was the driving force that kept me motivated in college.

As I matriculated through school, I desired to have a vehicle of my own to get back and forth from college to my hometown. I had to catch rides everywhere I went. I noticed that when I would ask others for rides, it would be as if I was inconveniencing them. After so many times experiencing the frustration of others being inconvenienced by me asking for a ride, I was determined to get my own vehicle.

The military recruiters would frequently visit the campus to recruit students to join. I would always resist them because I knew what my focus was. I knew that my goal would be greater than joining the military. Even though I resisted the recruiters, that didn't stop them from being aggressive and making offers I couldn't refuse. One day, I decided to go ahead and join the United States Marine Corps, but only as a reservist. By being a reservist, I could still be a student, play college football, and reach my goals.

Once I got to Paris Island, my life changed forever. All the lessons that life taught me came out in a way that I never knew was possible. Nothing could break me. Nothing that the drill instructors said shook me mentally. I was already broken. I was an overcomer. I had to overcome so much to have a normal life prior to joining the Marines. In recruit training, their whole goal was to break you down to build you up. All the things that transpired in my life had already fortified me. I was only there to make a better way for myself and to help my grandmother make ends meet while I was in college.

I wasn't the fastest, nor was I the smartest. All I had was determination, grit, and the knowledge that God was on my side. I was in a platoon of 70-plus recruits from all over the world. We all had one goal: Become United States Marines.

For three months, we watched no television, heard no music, and were not connected to the outside world by any means of technology. The only thing we did daily was submit ourselves to training and challenges that were designed to inflict pain upon us at a high level without killing us. This was nothing new to me. I trained at a high level back at home as an athlete. I was mentally prepared due to all the challenges that I had already overcome in my life. This was just another form of practice for me.

One day, the lead recruit of our platoon decided to do the wrong thing while no one was watching him. He was fast, strong, neat, and had all the outer attributes of a leader. There was one thing that was missing: integrity. One day, he decided to steal food from the cafeteria, sneak it into the squad bay, and put it into his footlocker. After being out all day running and training, we marched back to our squad bay to find out that our room was destroyed. All our mattresses were flipped over, and all our belongings were scattered across the floor. The drill instructors had checked our footlockers while we were away and found the food that the leader had stolen from the cafeteria.

After we spent hours doing pushups and running in place, our drill instructors made us clean up our squad bay and put everything back the way it was. While I was making up my bed, the drill instructor took the platoon mantle off the leader and came and threw it on my bunk while I was making my bed. He made me the leader! Immediately, my heart began to race. Fear began to fill my heart. I didn't possess the qualities needed to be a top recruit. I wasn't fast like the previous leader. I didn't have the endurance to run 8 miles at full speed, nor could I climb a rope. I had never climbed a rope in my life! All I had was determination. There was no way I could tell my drill instructor that I didn't want to be the leader; I accepted his choice and the challenge.

I led with humility and passion. I didn't let the position of top recruit go to my head because I knew there were other recruits who were faster and stronger than me. I knew I wasn't the only one that could lead us. I led as if I were just like the recruits who were following me. I was one of them, not better than them. Every moment I spent training, I would think about how proud my family would be once they saw me as a Marine. I would think about how I would be able to help my grandmother financially. That was my only motivation. My mind was fixed on that.

Every night before we went to bed, we would have a mail call. Our drill instructor would call us by our last names and have us run up and get our mail. I never received any mail. In fact, I was the only recruit who didn't receive any mail the entire time I was on the island. I didn't expect my grandmother to write me. She was older in age, and we both understood what my goals were prior to me leaving. I didn't have a girlfriend at the time. I was just focused on not being a failure in life. For three months, I led and never received any motivation from anyone on the outside. My motivation was my grandmother.

One day, while we were at the rifle range, my Senior Drill Instructor pulled me aside and asked me a question.

"Guide?"

"Yes, Sir," I replied.

"Relax because I need you to talk to me normally for a second," he said. "How do you get up every day, train hard, stay motivated, and give it your all while not getting any mail from anyone?" he asked.

"Sir, I'm only here to help my grandmother live a better life. I just want to be able to help her because she's done so much for me in my life. This was the only way I knew how to help her," I replied.

"I'm going to allow you to call home tonight, but don't tell anyone, or this could really affect my career," he replied.

He put his career on the line to give me favor and allow me to hear my grandmother's voice. While others may have received mail every day, I was able to hear the voice of my grandmother, and they never knew it. There's not too many Marines that have that testimony!

After three months of long, grueling training, we finally earned our Eagle, Globe, and Anchor. We were no longer recruits. We were United States Marines. I graduated top of my class and received the Governor's Award as the Honor Graduate in my Platoon. My aunt drove up, accompanied by my grandmother, my uncle, my sister, and my cousins. It was a proud moment that I will never forget. My grandmother cried tears of joy as she saw me for the first time in three months, standing out in front of hundreds of recruits worldwide. Everything that I have been through in life had prepared me for this moment. This moment showed everyone in my family, including myself, that it's not how you start in life, it's how you finish.

After graduation, I returned to Albany, where I was stationed, to get back into college and continue my quest to become a teacher, a professional football player, and now a United States Marine. As I returned for my sophomore year, I had the opportunity to walk on as a redshirt freshman with the Albany State University Football Team. The challenges didn't stop because I was accepted into school. I couldn't take the SAT because I didn't have a Certified Birth Certificate. Fortunately, I could take the Institutional SAT, which allowed me to test and become eligible only at the college I attended. I scored an 820 and was now eligible to play collegiate sports. I was so excited! I went through a week of tryouts and made the team.

Once I got on the team, I only had one goal: Be a starter! One day, while practicing on running routes and sprints on my own, there were scouts from the Oakland Raiders who were watching me train.

One of the scouts came over to me and encouraged me to keep working.

"We like your work ethic, and you never know where it will take you," he stated.

Even in my training, the things that my grandmother Rosa instilled in me were starting to manifest more fruit in my life. After redshirting and completing my developmental studies, I began to become more focused on building my speed and getting my weight back up, which I lost during Marine Corps Training, to play the running back position. The opportunity for me to start at running back was available for me, as the previous starter had graduated.

I purchased my first vehicle, which was a 1985 BMW, for $500. The owner of the vehicle was one of my professors who saw my work ethic and gave me favor by allowing me to purchase the vehicle by paying $100 dollars a month until I paid it off.

During the spring of my sophomore year, I got a job at McDonald's to make some cash to pay my insurance and have gas money to move around when I needed to. When I wasn't working, I was studying. When I wasn't at work or in classes, I was training. My life was simple: Train, work, study, excel in the classroom, hit the weight room, and rise to the occasion once the season starts.

One night, when I got home from work, I checked my voicemail messages on my dorm room phone.

"Pack up your bags, Marine. We're being deployed for active duty."

My reserve unit was called to active duty due to the terrorist attacks at the Twin Towers in 2001. I was shattered. All my dreams and aspirations were taken away from me. I had to leave college and become a full-time Marine. I never counted the cost of being a reservist and the possibility of having to leave school. I joined the Marines with the assumption that there would never be any war and we would never be deployed. Boy, was I wrong!

CHAPTER 12
God Brought Me Out

A s we deployed to Jacksonville, North Carolina, I fell into a deep depression. This was not the way that I planned for my life to go. Once we arrived at the base, we were placed in barracks with Marines that were already established. I ended up joining rooms with two Marines from Utah. One of the things my grandmother always taught me was to never judge a person by their color. She raised me to treat all people the way I want to be treated, and everything else would fall into place. Once we got to know each other, there was an immediate connection I forged with them.

Then, the unimaginable happened. They pulled out a bottle of alcohol.

"Hey, Marine, would you like to try some?" he asked.

"No, I'm good," I responded.

I continued to unpack my things and think about how my plans were derailed by something that I didn't have any control over. As the night continued, I saw the fun that they were having. I gave in to the temptation and asked them to pour me a drink. It was my first time drinking, and I was curious about how alcohol tasted, even though I had seen the effects of it growing up. Little did I know this drink would begin a downward spiral in my life.

This was my first time getting drunk. This experience impacted me in such a way, that I began purchasing my own alcohol after that night. Every day that I got off work, I would have drinks with my friends. Though I was having fun, in the back of my mind, I was disappointed in myself for giving in to temptation and going against the way I was raised. No one knew that I was heavily addicted to alcohol at this point. I went out to clubs every other day just to get my mind off the depression that I was in. I drank every day for the entire year we were stationed in North Carolina.

Once we completed deployment and returned to Albany, I was released to return to normalcy. I went from being in a wartime environment to living in the dorms with normal college students again. I came back to school with an alcohol addiction. I was so depressed that I couldn't walk into a classroom without feeling that someone knew I was an alcoholic. I decided to go and see a doctor about the feelings that I was having. I was diagnosed with PTSD and high blood pressure due to all the alcohol I was consuming. He prescribed me medicine to take, but being that I was young, I didn't take the medicine. I just kept drinking.

I decided to get my first apartment a few months after getting back from deployment to have my own living space. I was a young Active-Duty Marine with an addiction problem and no guidance. Instead of getting back on track and pursuing my initial plan, I became fascinated with the nightlife and the freedom that I had of being on my own and having my own place. One night, as I was out drinking and driving, I ran a stop sign going 55 MPH and hit a car on the driver's side. I flipped my car over and knocked the driver 20 yards away from the impact. It was only by the grace of God that I didn't kill the driver or myself. I went to jail for the first time in my life with a DUI charge.

I felt so ashamed and so low because this wasn't who I was raised to be. I had no guidance. Even though I was raised to always do the right thing, I lost my way due to having too much freedom and too much money at an early age. I grew up praising God and serving God, but at this moment in my life, I was serving my flesh. I was fortunate enough to get a pretrial diversion, which allowed me to pay a fine, serve community service time, and get my license back after one year.

This entire experience shook me to my core. I slowed down a bit, but not for long. I continued the path of destruction vicariously. After years of living a life of sin, I decided that it was time to give my life totally to God. I learned that your salvation as a child doesn't yield fruit if you're not living holy as a man. I woke up one Sunday morning and went to the first church I could find. After visiting many churches, I wasn't compelled to change my life, as I continued to drink and party on the weekends.

Then, one Wednesday evening in 2013, I decided to stop at a church called Rhema International Ministries. As I walked into the church, the first thing I noticed was the excellence on the grounds and the distinct scent of the church. The scent wrapped around me like a warm embrace, reminiscent of my aunt's living room. It carried a sense of responsibility, a comforting reminder of familiar ties. It felt like home.

I sat on the back row with no expectations from the Pastor, as I had been let down by every visit to other churches. All I knew was if I didn't make a change, I would be dead or in jail again soon. As soon as the Pastor opened his mouth and began to speak, I heard the voice of God! His passion for people to be blessed was like those who sacrificed for me to have a better life despite my beginnings. His love for God and the scriptures reminded me of my childhood Pastor. My heart leaped for joy because I knew my deliverance was going to come through this Man of God's mouth. His name is Pastor Scott Sanders.

As the service began, he preached from Matthew 11:28. That message was for me because I was tired of living the way I was. I was tired of living a life of sin that would eventually take me out. After the service was over, I decided that this was where I needed to be. I desired to join that night, but the invitation was not given. I drove home in tears of joy because I found a place where I could be accountable and embark on a journey that would change my life forever.

As I matured in the faith and allowed God to change me from the inside out, the things that I used to do were no longer appealing to me. I became more focused and less driven to fulfill the desires of my flesh. Day by day, I was being transformed by the Word of God. Through all the disappointments and the shame I faced over the years, falling in love with Jesus brought a wholeness into my life that I will cherish forever.

When I look back over my life and reflect on all the situations I was in, I realize that God was always there. He already had someone in place to ensure that I was covered. He already had someone in place with the keys to every chain that had me bound. His name is Jesus!

Today, I've recovered from being brokenhearted for most of my life. I've recovered from being a nicotine and weed addict. I've recovered from being an alcoholic and frequently going out to nightclubs. Today, I'm clean, and I live totally for God, which is how I was raised to be in the beginning. I'm married with a wonderful son and believing God for our first-born child together.

Regarding my mothers, my mother, Ladedra, passed away on April 6, 2015, and my grandmother, Virginia, passed away on May 5, 2015. As for my brothers, I'm still searching for them. I remember my grandmother encouraging me to have a hard conversation with my mother about my brothers. This wasn't the easiest conversation to have, as my Mother Ladedra was fighting to overcome cancer.

As my Mother Ladedra discussed what happened with my brothers, I could tell it was taking a toll on her body to talk about the details. I encouraged her that everything would be ok, and that God will make a way for us to find them. After the conversation, I told my mother these words. "I just want you to know that you're the best mother a son could ever have." "I never heard anything like that before Chip." She replied. I expressed to her that I forgave her for everything that transpired in our past. I explained to her that Jesus died for all our sins; past, present, and future. I expressed to her that just as Christ has redeemed us from the curse of the law, God's love made me see her as the best mother a man could ever have. "Thank you so much Chip. I needed that." She replied. Her thank you was filled with a peace that I would never forget. The next week, she transitioned to be with the Lord. Those were the last words that I spoke to her. I'm so grateful that I listened to my grandmother and was mature enough to love my mother at the most vulnerable moment of her life. We all need His Grace!

I didn't grow up with a silver spoon in my mouth, nor did I have all the resources I needed in the beginning to live a normal life as a child. I didn't make it to the NFL with a multimillion-dollar contract. But by God's grace and his goodness, I overcame poverty and received salvation. Every day, I desire more of God and his love.

Throughout my journey, I've discovered that even though I didn't have it all together, God ensured that everything worked together for my good. I could've given in and become what I saw in my environment, but the love of God raised me and caused me to break through every generational curse! God's Love didn't abandon me; it adopted me. Today, I'm whole, healthy, happy, and prosperous because of the wonder-working power of God's Love.

Made in the USA
Columbia, SC
05 December 2024

48453603R00072